the end of me

JOURNAL

Published in Louisville, Kentucky, by City on a Hill Studio.

Additional copies of this guide along with other *The End of Me* study resources may be purchased online at **www.cityonahillstudio.com**.

Scripture quotations are taken from the HOLY BIBLE: New International Version® Copyright © 1973, 1978, 1984 by International Bible Society (unless otherwise noted).

The publishers would like to thank Bahram Khayatpour for the writing and development of the content in this journal.

TABLE OF CONTENTS

WEEK
ONE

WEEK 1
DAY 1

*"Draw near to God
and he will draw near to you."*
James 4:8

Anytime one embarks on a new journey, there must be a destination set. In other words, we must know where we are going. This concept is understood for the most part by all of us when we talk about going on a trip, whether we are planning a trip around the world or just running up to the grocery store. However, it is something that we often overlook when it comes to the spiritual journeys we endeavor. Many times, we just jump in without having a destination in mind. Unfortunately, this often keeps us from getting all the benefits from the journey.

Today, as we start our journey and start moving towards getting to the end of ourselves, we want to set some goals. These goals will serve as our spiritual destinations. In the space below, write a note to God. Explain to Him why you have decided to take part in this study. Then share with Him what you hope to get out of this study. **Take some time and reflect on how you would like to be different at the end of this series. Then write**

that down in your note to God as well.

_____

_____

_____

_____

_____

_____

_____

_____

_____

_____

_____

_____

_____

Take some time to pray over the things you just wrote. Pray that God would lead, direct, and transform you in the next few weeks. Pray that you would have an open heart and an attentive mind to God's spirit moving in your heart and mind.

WEEK 1

DAY 2

*"Give thanks to the Lord,
for he is good: his love endures forever."*
Psalm 107:1

Jesus told us in John 14 that He has given us a guide in His Holy Spirit who lives in us. Jesus has also promised that He will never leave us or forsake us. He has told us over and over in the Gospels that He is always with us. Therefore, we know that we are never alone on our journeys. We know God is always with us, guiding and leading us. As great as that sounds, this is often a hindrance to people when it comes being honest with their brokenness. The reason for this is we often have a misguided view of God. We feel that He is a rule keeper judge who is ready to strike down against us if we do anything wrong. Therefore, this often keeps us from being completely transparent with our brokenness.

Today, we want to get a proper view of God and especially His love for us. **Look up the verses below. In the space next to each verse write down what that verse reveals to you about God's character.**

John 3:16: _____

Romans 8:38-39: _____

Psalm 103:8: _____

Jeremiah 31:3: _____

Revelation 21:4: _____

Psalm 103:10-12: _____

Romans 5:8: _____

Spend a few minutes looking over God's love for you. Spend some time in prayer and thank Him for being so good. You may want to thank Him for times He has specifically shown you some of the attributes you wrote down. Pray that God would help you be more open about your brokenness knowing that He is a good and loving God.

WEEK 1
DAY 3

" The LORD is near to the brokenhearted
And saves those who are crushed in spirit."
Psalm 34:18

Yesterday we set some goals for this series and this journey we are beginning through this series. Another important part of any journey is not only to know where you are going but to also know where you are. Many years ago most of us had a map in our cars and that is how we got around. Then came MapQuest and other online tools which mapped out your route for you. Today, most people have a GPS system either in their cars or on their phones. All you have to do is type in the address of your destination and it will guide you along the path. However, the address of your destination is only half of the vital information the GPS unit needs. The other half, and maybe the most important piece of information, is your current location. If the GPS unit does not know where you currently are located, it cannot help you get to your destination even when it knows the exact location of your destination. This same concept rings true in our spiritual journeys. Although we know where we want to go we must be honest with where we are. We will never get to where we want to go, if we do not know where we are.

Today, we are going to be honest about our current condition. This is the first step to getting to the "end of me". As we learned in the study, we are all broken. However, it is only when we are honest with the state of our brokenness that we truly have a proper understanding of our current condition. Take a few minutes and spend some time in silence with God. As you are still, ask God to reveal your brokenness. Remember, God is the most loving, graceful, forgiving, etc., being in the universe and He loves you just the way you are.

When you are finished, move down to the outline below. The person outlined below represents you and your life. **Write your name on the line inside the person. Then write down words that would describe your current condition and the state of your current brokenness inside the person.** Again, this exercise is not meant to bring guilt or shame, rather help us be honest with God and ourselves so that we can plan out our journey to wholeness appropriately.

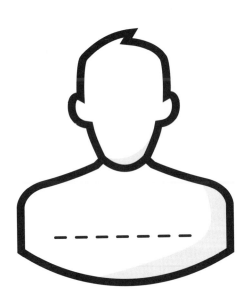

Spend a few minutes looking over your picture. Take some time as you pray and thank God for His love, grace, forgiveness and acceptance. Remember that those words do not define you and more importantly remember that those words will never make God love you any less!

WEEK 1
DAY 4

*"As the heavens are higher than
the earth, so are my ways higher than
your ways and my thoughts than your thoughts."*
Isaiah 55:9

Perspective changes everything. Have you ever seen one of those images that are meant to play "tricks" on your eyes. They'll ask you - what do you see, an old lady, or a rabbit? At first, all you can see is one of the images. But if you change your focus, sometimes you can see the other.

Just like these images, we often only look at our lives through one perspective: our own. We don't realize that there is another perspective. There is a better perspective. An Eternal perspective. Today, we are going to look at our lives from God's point of view. You see the problem with our perspective is that it is limited. One way we limit ourselves is we often define ourselves by the things we have done. This is not the way God sees us. Take some time and go over the verses below.

What God says about YOU:

God's **child** (John 1:12)

a **friend** of Jesus Christ (John 15:15)

justified (Romans 5:1)

united with the Lord

one with Him in spirit (1 Cor. 6:17)

a **member** of Christ's body (1 Cor. 12:27)

chosen and **adopted** (Ephesians 1:3-8)

redeemed and **forgiven** (Colossians 1:13-14)

complete (Colossians 2:9-10)

FREE from condemnation (Romans 8:1-2)

established, anointed, and **sealed** by God (2 Cor. 1:21-22)

hidden with Christ (Colossians 3:1-4)

a **citizen** of Heaven (Philippians 3:20)

the **branch** of Jesus Christ, the true vine, and a **channel** of His life (John 15:5)

chosen and **appointed** to bear fruit (John 15:16)

God's **temple** (1 Cor. 3:16)

a **minister** of reconciliation for God (2 Cor. 5:17-21)

seated with Jesus Christ (Ephesians. 2:6)

and **God's workmanship** (Ephesians. 2:10)

Take some time and reflect on each statement. This is how God sees you! In the space below write down your thoughts and feelings. How does it make you feel that God sees you like this?

_____

_____

_____

_____

_____

How does seeing God's view of you change the way you see yourself?

_____

_____

_____

_____

_____

How does understanding God's view of you encourage you to live differently?

_____

_____

_____

_____

_____

Take a few minutes and pray. Ask God to help you view yourself more like He views you. Ask Him to help you see others this way as well. Spend some time thanking God for His goodness.

WEEK 1
DAY 5

"I, even I, am he who blots out your transgressions,
for my own sake, and remembers your sins no more."
Isaiah 43:25

Colossians 3:3 says *"your life is hidden in Christ."* Since our lives are hidden in Christ, it means when God looks down on us, he sees Jesus. In theology there is a term called "double imputation." The word imputation means that it has been placed upon you. For instance the Bible says when Jesus died on the cross, he took all of our sins and brokenness upon himself. In other words, when God looked down at Jesus on the cross, He saw Jesus as if He had lived your life. This is imputation. Our sins and lives was imputed on Jesus. Most Christians understand this concept since it a core belief of Christianity. However, one thing that is often overlooked is that there was another imputation. The Bible teaches us that at the same time as our brokenness was placed on Jesus, Jesus' righteousness was placed on us. This is how we are hidden in Christ.

Grab a marker (preferably a red one). Revelation 1:5 says "...*Jesus Christ, who is the faithful witness, the firstborn from the dead, and the ruler of the kings of the earth. To him who loves us and has freed us from our sins by his blood....*" It is because of Jesus' shed blood that we are now hidden in Him. Turn back to the picture with the broken words you wrote on Day 3. Take the marker, which represents Jesus, and color in yourself with Jesus. As you do this, let the truth that God has covered all your sins and brokenness resound in your mind. Take some time and reflect on the fact that all your junk, sins, and brokenness is covered by Jesus.

In the following space, answer the questions...

How does it make you feel that Jesus took upon Himself all your sins, shame, and brokenness?

_____

_____

_____

_____

_____

_____

_____

How does it make you feel that you are hidden in Christ?

_____

_____

_____

_____

_____

_____

How does the fact that you are hidden in Christ, help you embrace your brokenness and ultimately come to the end of yourself?

_____

_____

_____

_____

_____

"Praise be to the God and Father of our Lord Jesus Christ, the Father of compassion and the God of all comfort, who comforts us in all our troubles, so that we can comfort those in any trouble with the comfort we ourselves receive from God."
2 Corinthians 1: 3-4

"God never wastes a hurt!" That is one of the greatest truths I have ever heard. As followers of Jesus, our brokenness is never in vain. Romans 8:28 tells us that God uses everything for good when we are His followers. It brings us hope knowing that God uses our pains to continue to mold us into the people we were always meant to be.

God also uses our brokenness to help others who are broken. 2 Corinthians 1:4 teaches us that God comforts us in our pains so that we can comfort others. Dealing with our pain and brokenness is never easy. However, one of the greatest ways God brings us encouragement in our brokenness is to use us to help others who are broken.

Think of someone who is broken. Since all of us are broken, this could be anyone. However, you may want to choose someone who is going through an especially hard time right now. **Get a piece of paper or a card and write a note of encouragement to that person.** In the note, remind them of how much God loves them. You can share with them how God has comforted you during difficult time. You may want to share some of the insights or verses you gave learned by going through this study.

Once you have completed your note, spend some time praying for that person. Pray that God would reveal His love to him/her in an incredible way. Pray that your card would help him/her embrace their brokenness and find God's love at the end of himself/herself.

WEEK 1
DAY 7

"Blessed are the poor in spirit,
for theirs is the kingdom of heaven."
Matthew 5:3

 s we finish this first week of our study on the "End of Me", today we are going to take some time to reflect on what God has been teaching us.

Take some time and go back through the first 6 days of this journal.

What is one thing you have learned about God this week?

_____

_____

_____

_____

_____

_____

What is one think you have learned about yourself this week?

_____

_____

_____

_____

_____

_____

What is one thing you can start to implement in your life in order to move toward the end of you?

_____

_____

_____

_____

_____

Prayer is the foundation of a healthy and strong spirituality. One group of Christians who modeled the practice of prayer were the Puritans. It has been written about them that the strength of their character was forged through their lives of prayer and meditation. For the Puritans, prayer was of first importance to life and spirituality. Due to this foundation of prayer they often had very impactful and inspiring prayer. Below is a puritan prayer called "Yet I Sin." This prayer very much embodies what this week has been all about. It is a prayer of coming to the end of ourselves and surrendering to God.

We are going to end every week by spending some time with God though the exercise of prayer. As you begin your prayer time, read the prayer below to God. Pray it to God as if it was your prayer to Him. Then spend 5-10 minutes in silence as you listen for God's spirit to move within you. Finally end your time by wording your own prayer to God.

"Yet I Sin"

Eternal Father,
Thou art good beyond all thought,
But I am vile, wretched, miserable, blind;
My lips are ready to confess,
but my heart is slow to feel,
and my ways reluctant to amend.
I bring my soul to thee;
break it, wound it, bend it, mould it.
Unmask to me sin's deformity,
that I may hate it, abhor it, flee from it.

My faculties have been a weapon of revolt
against thee;
as a rebel I have misused my strength,
and served the foul adversary of thy kingdom.
Give me grace to bewail my insensate folly,
Grant me to know that the way of transgressors
is hard, that evil paths are wretched paths,
that to depart from thee is to lose all good.

I have seen the purity and beauty of thy perfect law,
the happiness of those in whose heart it reigns,
the calm dignity of the walk to which it calls,
yet I daily violate and contemn its precepts.

Thy loving Spirit strives within me,
brings me Scripture warnings,
speaks in startling providences,

allures by secret whispers,
yet I choose devices and desires to my own hurt,
impiously resent, grieve,
and provoke him to abandon me.
All these sins I mourn, lament, and for them cry pardon.

Work in me more profound and abiding repentance;
Give me the fullness of a godly grief
that trembles and fears,
yet ever trusts and loves,
which is ever powerful, and ever confident;
Grant that through the tears of repentance
I may see more clearly the brightness
and glories of the saving cross.

———————

WEEK
TWO

the end of me

DAY 8

"Blessed are those who mourn,
for they will be comforted."
Matthew 5:4

Not too long ago, a new song hit the airways called "Happy" by Pharrell Williams. It did not take long for "Happy" to rise to #1 on the charts. It was constantly on the radio, at parties, in movies, at weddings and in commercials. I think one of the reasons that song became so big, so fast is because our culture is obsessed with being happy. It seems like people's actions are motivated by a desire to remain happy. We have believed the lie that the key to a good life is to be happy all the time. Now this concept is not really possible and actually not the best, but we will deal with that later.

Not only has our culture mislead us to believe that we should be happy all the time, but even the idea of what makes us happy has been falsified. The things that we believe will make us happy end up either being temporary or not making us happy at all.

One of the very first things Jesus does after he begins his earthly ministry is to correct our earthly thinking by teaching us how things work in his kingdom. Through the beatitudes, Jesus takes everything we know about living and happiness and turns them upside down. Jesus often does this throughout his ministry. In fact, one of my favorite terms for God's kingdom is the "Upside Down" kingdom.

So when it comes to happiness, Jesus tells us it is not found in many of the things we are seeking. He tells us that it is found in relationships, forgiveness, growth, sacrifice, serving, others, maturity, and ultimately in following him.

What does our culture tell us about what makes us happy?

_____

_____

_____

_____

Spend some time thinking about the happiest times of your life. In the space below give an overview of what those times were.

Happy Experience #1:

_____

_____

Happy Experience #2:

_____

_____

Happy Experience #3:

_____

_____

As you reminisce about those times, try to think what makes them such happy memories for you. Were there any special circumstances which made them a happy memory?

As you continue to think about the truly memorable times in your life, how are they more in line with what Jesus taught about happiness than what our culture tells us?

_____

_____

_____

_____

Take some time to connect and pray to God. Pray and thank him for the memorable times in your life. Thank him for being good and allowing us to experience the happy and joyful times in life. Pray that God would continue to give you his perspective so that you can view happiness and joy in the correct way and therefore be able to find more happiness in all your circumstances.

"Then Jacob awoke from his sleep and said, "Surely the Lord is in this place, and I did not know it." He was afraid and said, "How awesome is this place! This is none other than the house of God, and this is the gate of heaven." So Jacob rose early in the morning, and took the stone that he had put under his head and set it up as a pillar and poured oil on its top."
Genesis 28:16-18

We have all heard (and possible used!) the phrase "What have you done for me lately?" when talking to God. This seems to be one of the failings of the human condition: we tend to have short memories. It is nothing new. It has been a flaw of humanity for thousands of years. In fact, when we read the scripture, especially the Old Testament, we notice that this human forgetfulness is something they were well aware of about themselves.

You may have noticed that many times throughout the scriptures, we will read about a person who has an encounter with God. Immediately after this encounter the person would build an altar to represent their encounter. The altars were usually made up of some rocks and would normally be a couple of feet high. The reason they did this was as practical as spiritual. The people of that time would often travel from one town to the next to trade goods. Therefore, the routes they walked were common, repeated at least a couple times a month and throughout the year. So these altars would be something that they would see from time to time as they traveled. And immediately they would be reminded of the time God showed up in their lives.

You see, God's people knew their tendency to forget about what God had done in their past and have a "what have you done for me lately?" attitude towards God. Therefore, they would build these altars as a reminder.

We too have short memories. This not only hurts our attitude towards God, but makes it more difficult to get through times of mourning and suffering. In times of mourning, one of the greatest comforts and encouragements is the fact that God has delivered us through difficult times in the past.

Today we are going to build some symbolic altars in our lives. Take some time and reflect on some past trials that you have gone through. What was the situation? How did you feel entering the trial? How did God comfort you and show up in the midst of your mourning? Write down your experience below.

Trial:

_____

_____

How God comforted you:

_____

_____

_____

_____

Trial:

_____

_____

How God comforted you:

_____

_____

Trial:

_____

_____

How God comforted you:

_____

_____

_____

_____

Now we are going to make some altars. Find some rocks that will serve as a representation of God comforting you in the past. Find one rock for each trial God carried you through. Put the rocks either on top of each other if possible, or in a pile next to each other. It is a good idea to place your altar in a place where you would see it on a regular basis. It is never easy to go through difficult times, but when we can look back and see how God has carried us through times of mourning in the past, we become much more hopeful that He will carry us through this as well.

"All Scripture is breathed out by God and profitable for teaching, for reproof, for correction, and for training in righteousness, that the man of God may be competent, equipped for every good work."
2 Timothy 3:16-17

One of the greatest tools God has given us as we follow him is his word. Through his word, God describes his love for us, his plans for us, he character, and so much more. Through his word, we are given hope, peace, encouragement, purpose, strength and so much more! Unfortunately, for many people, those same scriptures that are meant to give us encouragement and hope are very distant. It is easy to think the scriptures are about other people who lived a long, long time ago. We misunderstand that although the stories are based on people in history, they are meant to be intimate, personal expressions from God to each of us.

The Bible is such an encouraging and hopeful resource for us when we are dealing with times of suffering and mourning. However, we need to experience the scriptures in a very personal way in order to truly gain that hope and encouragement. Below you will find one of the most encouraging pieces of scriptures when dealing with difficult times. Psalm 23 has been recited and memorized for generations because of its focus on God's comfort in the midst of trying times. **Read Psalm 23. Then write your name in all the places with an underlined space.** Now read Psalm 23 personalized with your name. Read it out loud and emphasize your name. Try to be conscious of the fact that God is speaking to you through this Psalm.

The Lord is _____'s shepherd, _____ lacks nothing.
He makes _____ lie down in green pastures,
he leads _____ beside quiet waters, he refreshes
_____'s soul.

He guides _____ along the right paths for his name's sake.
Even though _____ walks through the darkest valley,
_____ will fear no evil, for you are with _____;
your rod and your staff, they comfort _____.
You prepare a table before _____
in the presence of _____'s enemies.

You anoint _____'s head with oil;
_____'s cup overflows.
Surely your goodness and love will follow _____
all the days of _____'s life,
and _____ will dwell in the
house of the Lord forever.

Spend some time in prayer as you thank God for being your shepherd. Thank him for his ever present presence in your life. Thank him for leading and guiding you during good times as well as during difficult times. End your prayer by asking him to continually remind you of his personal care, love and comfort for you.

"Very truly I tell you, unless a kernel of wheat falls to the ground and dies, it remains only a single seed. But if it dies, it produces many seeds."
John 12:24

As you look around and observe the way the world and our lives work, it does not take long to realize that there is a certain rhythm and cycle to life. There is a cycle to our days, weeks, months, years and so on. We see this cycle in our seasons. We see this cycle in the basics of life. This rhythm teaches us so much about life. One of the truths we learn in this cycle is the fact that in order to have new life, other things must die. There is no greater example of this than in Jesus. We know it is through Jesus' death that anyone who puts their faith in him will have life. Without God there is no life.

This concept is true in our eternal lives, but it is also true for our lives here on earth. As God continually prunes us and molds us into the image of his son Jesus, there are things in our lives that must die. Although this may be a simple concept, it is still difficult! Dying to self is not an easy thing. Coming to the end of ourselves is often painful. However, it is much more appealing when we start realizing that God wants to create something new in us through the death of our flesh.

Today's exercise is designed to help us understand the beauty that God creates out of coming to the end of ourselves. Go outside and find a place where you can observe God's creation. Look around at the beauty of God's creation. Try to stay focused and take in all of it. Answer the questions below as you observe.

Describe do you see:

_____

_____

_____

_____

What beauty do you see in each object?

_____

_____

_____

_____

_____

_____

_____

_____

Now take some time and reflect on the idea that all the beauty that you see is a result of some sort of death. Now in the space below write down how death has brought beauty in the things that you are looking at.

_____

_____

_____

_____

_____

Take a few minutes to thank God for his amazing creation. Pray and ask him to remind you that you too are his beautiful creation. Ask him to remind you that he wants to bring some beautiful things into fruition in you. Finally ask him to give you strength to let go of the things that need to die in your life.

DAY 12

"I want to know Christ—yes, to know the power of his resurrection and participation in his sufferings, becoming like him in his death, and so, somehow, attaining to the resurrection from the dead."
Philippians 3:10-11

In the first book of the Bible we learn that we are created in God's image. Since then, sin has entered the world and distorted us; but we still resemble God in many ways. One of the ways we resemble God is in our parenting. Parents have plans for their kids. They have hopes and dreams that their child would grow up to be the best they can be. This is also true of God. God has plans for each of his children. Through his word, God tells us that he has good plans for us. His desire for us is to grow to be the best we can be. And the best we can be is to become more like Jesus. As God transforms us into the image of Jesus, we become the best version of ourselves.

Now this all works well until God's goal for us goes against our desire to be free from pain. All of us have a desire to be free from pain. All of us have a desire to be happy. God wants this for us as well. However, God knows that growth does not always happen in this kind of environment. In fact, quite the opposite is true. Most growth happens in times of mourning and suffering. There have been many surveys done about the subject of spiritual growth and although they vary in a lot of things, one thing remains true for almost all of the people surveyed. It turns out that the greatest times of spiritual growth for most people occurs during times of mourning and suffering. And since God's greatest goal for us it to grow and transform into the image of Jesus, it means sometimes he will allow us to go through times of pain and suffering. But the key is that he will use your mourning to mold and shape you into the image of his son, Jesus.

Below are some of the things Jesus endured and experienced through his earthly ministry. Go through the list and check which of the things you have also experienced.

☐ *Rejected by his family*
☐ *Rejected by his own people*
☐ *Rejected by everyone*
☐ *Betrayed by his close friend*
☐ *Death of family and friends*
☐ *Persecuted*
☐ *Beaten*
☐ *Arrested*
☐ *Died*
☐ *Lied to*
☐ *Falsely accused*
☐ *Separated from father*
☐ *Forsaken*
☐ *Mistreated*
☐ *Hated*

Look over the boxes you checked. Because of your trials, you now have more in common with Jesus. He knows what it is like to feel the way you did in your times of suffering. And you know what it is like to feel the way he did in those times as well. Take some time to reflect on how you know Jesus a little more because of your suffering. In the space below write down some of your thoughts on this subject.

How does it make you feel knowing that you know Jesus more intimately because of your suffering?

_____

_____

_____

_____

In what ways have you seen God use your times of suffering not just to know Jesus more, but to be more like him?

_____

_____

_____

_____

Spend some time in prayer as you thank God for not only seeing you through your trials but actually using them to make you more like Jesus. Pray that God would remind you that the temporary pain you feel in your trials is being used to make you eternally more like Jesus.

"This Book of the Law shall not depart from your mouth, but you shall meditate on it day and night, so that you may be careful to do according to all that is written in it. For then you will make your way prosperous, and then you will have good success."
Joshua 1:8

Times of suffering and mourning are often associated with darkness. It is often in these times when the world does not seem to shine as bright as it once did. The sun does not seem to warm your skin as it did before. Colors are not as vibrant. Food often loses its taste and even the roses do not seem as fragrant. Everything seems darker. It is in these times that we need to cling to God and his word the most. Psalm 119:105 says, "Your word is a lamp unto my feet." It is God's holy word that leads us along the path when it is dark. It is the scriptures that will guide us through the darkness back to the light.

When we read and are reminded of God's promises, we realize that our despair is not as deep as we thought. We remember that God is with us in the darkness. Through his word we remember that he is faithful and will not forget his promises to us. Ultimately, It is through his word that the light of hope once again shines in our hearts and minds.

Unfortunately, it is during trials that we tend to ignore or forget the things we need the most. During dark times, we often neglect the lamp that has been given to us. The Bible tells us to keep God's word on our hearts and minds. Today we are going to do an exercise to help us remember God's promises throughout the day. Take 5 notecards (or cut a piece of paper into 5 pieces). On each notecard write out one of the verses below. You will write one card for every verse.

Revelation 21:4 - *"And God will wipe away every tear from their eyes; there shall be no more death, nor sorrow, nor crying. There shall be no more pain, for the former things have passed away."*

Jeremiah 29:11 - *"For I know the thoughts that I think toward you, says the LORD, thoughts of peace and not of evil, to give you a future and a hope."*

Isaiah 41:10 - *"Fear not, for I am with you; be not dismayed, for I am your God; I will strengthen you, I will help you, I will uphold you with my righteous right hand."*

Psalm 9:9-10 - *"The LORD is a stronghold for the oppressed, a stronghold in times of trouble. And those who know your name put their trust in you, for you, O LORD, have not forsaken those who seek you."*

John 16:33 – *"I have said these things to you, that in me you may have peace. In the world you will have tribulation. But take heart; I have overcome the world."*

When you are done, take out your phone or your watch. Set your alarm to go off every 2 hours. The goal is to carry these cards with you throughout your day. Every time your alarm goes off, take out one of the cards and read them. When you read them, go slow and take the words in. This will help keep the promises on your mind throughout the day. Feel free to take them out more frequently if you desire.

WEEK 2
DAY 14

"More than that, we rejoice in our sufferings, knowing that suffering produces endurance, and endurance produces character, and character produces hope, and hope does not put us to shame, because God's love has been poured into our hearts through the Holy Spirit who has been given to us."
Romans 5:3-5

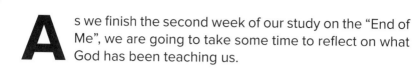

As we finish the second week of our study on the "End of Me", we are going to take some time to reflect on what God has been teaching us.

Take some time and go back through the past 6 days of this journal.

What is one thing you have learned about God this week?

_____

_____

_____

_____

_____

What is one thing you have learned about yourself this week?

_____

_____

_____

_____

_____

What is one thing you can start to implement in your life in order to move toward the end of you?

_____

_____

_____

_____

The apostle Paul said in Philippians 3:10-11, *"I want to know Christ—yes, to know the power of his resurrection and participation in his sufferings, becoming like him in his death, and so, somehow, attaining to the resurrection from the dead."* Paul understood that as he suffered like Jesus, God was going to mold him to look and act more like Jesus. Therefore, the apostle Paul welcomed coming to the end of himself.

That is the goal for us as well. The goal is not just to be able to endure times of mourning, because we know that God is with us. Not just to get through times of suffering because we know God is using it to shape our hearts and minds. But the goal is that we would come to understand how amazing it is to be transformed into the likeness of Christ that we would actually welcome suffering in our lives. That we would come to the end of ourselves, knowing that there is a special blessing found only there.

In the space below, write out your own prayer to God when it comes to enduring pain and suffering. Write an honest prayer about where you are in this area and where you want to be.

_____

_____

_____

_____

_____

_____

_____

_____

_____

_____

Finish by taking a few minutes to read your prayer to God.

WEEK
THREE

the end of me

WEEK 3
DAY 15

"He must become greater; I must become less." The one who comes from above is above all; the one who is from the earth belongs to the earth, and speaks as one from the earth. The one who comes from heaven is above all.'
John 3:30-31

Have you noticed there are two kinds of people in the world when it comes to putting gas in the car? There are the ones who wait for the last possible moment before they pull into the gas station. They know exactly how many miles they have when the little light comes, on signifying they are low on gas. It's is like a personal challenge for them every time that light comes on. They want to see how long they can go without getting stranded on the side of the road.

And then there are the other type of people. These people start having panic attacks anytime the gas needle drops below the half way point. These people wont ever get close to the light coming on in their own cars but when they are in someone else's car and the light comes on...look out. They start asking questions like "did you notice your gas light is on?" or "are you going to get gas anytime soon?" Then they start pointing out every gas station you drive by. If you look close enough, you can even see the fear in their eyes.

Even though we are all different when it comes to filling our cars with gas, I believe that most of us fall into the second category when it comes to filling our hearts and souls.

None of us like to feel empty in our souls. So we fill ourselves with whatever we can, to make sure we are always on full. Some get their fill through achievement and success. Others in riches and monetary possessions. Still others fill their souls with status. The list of fillers goes on and on. The problem with all of them is that they do not satisfy. The irony and sad truth is that most people spend their entire lives striving to fill themselves with things that only end up making them feel even more empty.

The fact is that we were all created to live through and live with our creator. We were designed to live in communion with God. And when we are not living in close community with Him, being filled by Him, we feel empty. And even though we fill ourselves with everything other than God, it will never satisfy. On the flipside when we fill ourselves up with Him alone, we are completely satisfied and filled. However, most of us are already so full of the stuff that doesn't satisfy that there is hardly any room left for Him.

Take some time and think of all the stuff you fill yourself with. These are the earthly things you get your worth from. They are the things you think you'll find your purpose in, aside from God. They are the things you strive for, but end up never

fully satisfying. Write them down in the space below.

_____

_____

_____

_____

_____

_____

_____

_____

_____

_____

_____

_____

_____

Once you are done writing down all the things you fill yourself with, grab a drinking glass and a couple pieces of paper. Take the paper and cut it in half length wise as well as width wise. This should create eight smaller pieces of paper. Write down each of the things you wrote above on each piece of paper. Then go ahead and crumple the paper up into a ball and place them one by one in the glass. The glass represents you in this exercise. Look and see how much of the glass is filled with your fillers. That is all space that could be filled with God. Please keep this glass with the paper inside it somewhere as a reminder this week of our need to be emptied in order to be filled by God.

Spend some time praying over your list. Pray that God would reveal to you how these never satisfy. Pray that you would realize that true satisfaction comes only by being filled with Jesus. Pray that God would help you start letting go so He can fill you with more of Himself.

DAY 16

"And to know the love of Christ that surpasses knowledge,
that you may be filled with all the fullness of God."
Ephesians 3:19

There is a story in the book of Ezekiel about four lepers who are stuck outside the city gate. The Bible does not tell us how long they have been there but we can know it was probably a good amount of time. At that time period people with leprosy were banished to live outside the city gates. They relied on the trash of the city, which was thrown outside the gate, for their food. Since the city had been in a famine, these lepers didn't have any trash to rummage through. Finally, one day they decided they could not live like this any longer. They said to each other, "If we stay here we will surely die." They end up going to another camp, and upon arriving, found that it had been deserted and there was a feast left behind!

The lepers decided they were tired of living the way they were and changed. And it saved their lives. We too often settle for leftovers and trash to fill us rather than the presence of the creator of the universe. We do this because we are just used to it. We don't realize that there is a better way, that God's way is better. We are scared to move because this is all we have ever known. This way of living is familiar to us. We don't know how good the alternative really is. But just like the lepers, if we continue to settle for the fillers that will never satisfy, we too will slowly die from the inside out.

We must realize that there is a treasure waiting for us as well. This treasure is not silver nor gold but the very presence of the almighty God. When we are filled with God, we are always satisfied. We are refreshed. We are strengthened. We are filled!

Again, one of the main reasons we continue to fill ourselves up with things that never satisfy is because we don't understand how good it is to be filled by God. **Look up each of the verses below. Next to each verse, write down the qualities that come as a result of being filled by God according to that verse.**

Matthew 11:28-29

_____

_____

_____

Jeremiah 17:8

_____

_____

_____

Psalm 1:3

_____

_____

_____

John 7:37-39

_____

_____

_____

In the spaces below, write down your current life circumstances that you recognize could use the qualities above:

Matthew 11:28-29- _____

Jeremiah 17:8- _____

Psalm 1:3- _____

John 7:37-39- _____

"Jesus answered, "Everyone who drinks this water will be thirsty again, but whoever drinks the water I give them will never thirst. Indeed, the water I give them will become in them a spring of water welling up to eternal life."
John 4:13-14

Jesus is a gentleman! He doesn't knock down doors. He doesn't force his way in. He waits until he is invited. In Revelation 3:20, Jesus says "Here I am! I stand at the door and knock. If anyone hears my voice and opens the door, I will come in and eat with that person, and they with me." As much as he desires to be with us and fill us with himself, he does not force his way in. He waits until we have made space for him. When we have made a place for him at the table of our hearts, he will gladly come in and fill us. But until then, he will politely wait outside and knock.

I have heard it said, "The greatest act of love is the fact that God has given us the ability to choose him." God does not want us to be robots. He wants us to lovingly and freely choose him. But this is not possible unless we have a choice. It is only when we are given a choice to NOT choose God, that we can truly choose to love him. It is easy to think of this concept as one that only applies to someone who has not accepted Jesus. However, that would be wrong. In the Revelation passage, Jesus is speaking to churches. To his followers. Because the ability to choose Jesus is a daily one for us as well.

Every day we ask, "Who or what will satisfy and fill me?" Are we going to be filled with earthly, temporal, created things? Or are we going to choose to be filled with the almighty creator? Remember, he is standing right there. He is knocking and waiting. He desires to fill us. But we must make room for him.

Grab your glass filled with the papers which represent the stuff you tend to fill yourself with. Take some time and take them out one by one. Open each piece of paper and read the filler written on it. Spend some time praying over it. Pray that God would give you the courage and strength to empty yourself of that filler. As you pray, try to visualize letting go of that filler. Picture your soul being empty of the need for that filler. Picture God replacing the space left void with His presence. Then physically get rid of the paper. You can rip it up to small pieces and throw it away. You may even want to burn it. The point is to physically get rid of it as a symbolic gesture of getting rid of it in your soul. Do this until your glass is empty. Once your glass is empty, go and fill it with water.

In the scriptures, water is used as a symbol for purity, refreshment, and life. It is also used as a symbol for God's presence. Take a few minutes and reflect on the fact that God desires to fill us with his pure, life giving, soul refreshing spirit and as you empty yourself, even now, he is already filling you with himself!

"Set your minds on things above,
not on earthly things."
Colossians 3:2

A couple of months ago I was working on a document on my computer. Once I finished I did what we all do, I saved my paper. Well...I tried to save my paper. My computer kept telling me that there was an error and my file could not be saved at that time. I tried over and over again but no luck. I did not understand what was going on. Since I am not a computer expert, I asked my friend, who happens to be an IT expert to take a look. It didn't take him long to find the problem. It turns out that my hard drive was full. There was no more space available on my computer, hence why my computer was unable to save the file. My first thought was "That's impossible!" I was immediately reminded of the day the computer was given to me. I remembered how it had some amazing number of gigabytes and how I had told myself at the time that there was no way I would ever fill that much space. My friend assured me that it was and showed me that indeed my hard drive was full.

It is incredible how quickly we can fill spaces with stuff. Whether it is a computer hard drive, closet, garage, or our minds. Throughout the scriptures God tells us over and over again, to keep him on our minds. There are many sources of mind clutter in world. A few common sources are: saying yes to too many things, anxiousness about finances, modern technology, social media, and our concern over what others think of us. All of these influences have a way of cluttering our minds. It is so easy to race through the maze of the day, allowing the world's ideals and our insecurities to clutter thoughts.

Philippians 4:8 says "Finally, brothers and sisters, whatever is true, whatever is noble, whatever is right, whatever is pure, whatever is lovely, whatever is admirable—if anything is excellent or praiseworthy—think about such things." The unfortunate truth is that we have so much stuff occupying our thoughts that we often don't have room to think of godly things. Pastor Charles Swindoll once said, "Too much clutter in your mind leaves insufficient room for devotion to Christ." So a part of emptying ourselves is to de-clutter our minds.

Look at the picture on the next page. Take 5-15 minutes writing down all the things that consume your thoughts in the thought bubbles. Take a marker and draw an "X" over all the things that you could live without. After doing this, look at the paper. What would your life look like if you spent more of your time being devoted to the things left on the paper?

Spend some time in prayer. Pray that God would continue to reveal to you all the things that clutter your mind. Pray that God would show you the things you can put out of your mind. Pray about ways you can slowly remove these things from your life.

WEEK 3
DAY 19

" Jesus answered, It is written:
'Man shall not live on bread alone, but on
every word that comes from the mouth of God.'"
Matthew 4:4

One of the greatest ways to be filled by God is to be filled with his word. Throughout the history of Christianity, God's word has been vital for spiritual growth. Today, in the US, we have more access to God's word than any other time in history. For most of Christian history, most people were illiterate. Up until the invention of the printing press in 1440, access to a Bible was extremely difficult and extremely expensive. Today, not only do we have affordable access to Bibles, but we have access to several different translations. The Bible is printed in several languages. We can read the Bible online or even on our phones.

Unfortunately, the wide access to God's word comes with a downfall. We often take God's word for granted. Since it is so available, we neglect it. Sometimes, the problem is not accessibility but information overload. We have the entire scriptures at our disposal. The Bible is comprised of 66 books, with over 1,100 chapters and over 31,000 verses. If that seems overwhelming to you, remember what one of my seminary professors used to say: "It doesn't matter that you get all the way through the Bible, it matters that the Bible gets all the way through to you."

For most of history, Christians did not have access to a complete Bible. They would often have pieces of scripture. A book, chapter or just a few verses. But they cherished those verses. They memorized and they lived them out. They were filled with them. Today, to help us focus and be filled with God's word, we are going to take part in the practice of repetition. Read the verses below. Choose the one that most speaks to you. Write it below in the space given.

Matthew 5:6
John 14:23
Acts 2:28
Ephesians 1:22-23
Ezekiel 37:27

_____

Verse

_____

_____

_____

Spend five minutes just reflecting on the verse. What does it mean? What is God saying to you personally through it? What would it look like if your life embodied this verse?

Spend the next five minutes repeating the verse to yourself. As you read, think about God filling you with His presence. Try to visualize God filling you more and more every time you repeat the verse.

Spend the next five minutes praying the verse. Read it out loud adding words to make it a prayer to God.

WEEK 3
DAY 20

"Do not lay up for yourselves treasures on earth, where moth and rust destroy and where thieves break in and steal, but lay up for yourselves treasures in heaven, where neither moth nor rust destroys and where thieves do not break in and steal."
Matthew 6:19-20

The ancient Jews did not have the word "spiritual" in their language. They believed if some things were labeled spiritual, it would mean that others would be considered "not spiritual." This was simply something they did not believe. They believed that everything was spiritual. Every thing, every act, and every person was somehow connected to God and therefore spiritual.

Today, we live in a world that views things very differently than the ancient Jews. We see almost everything as spiritual or non-spiritual. Unfortunately, this is a mistake. Often times, the physical is tied to the spiritual. This is why God tells us we must love Him with all of our heart, mind, soul and strength, which is another way of saying physical body. John 4:24 reminds us that we must worship God in spirit and in truth.

One way to empty ourselves spiritually is to let go of physical things. Especially in our materialistic culture, our identities are often tied to our physical stuff more than we know. So to help empty ourselves on every level, we need to rid ourselves of these things.

Go through your home and look around at all the "stuff "you own. What do you have that you can give away. It may be something you have not used in years. It may be something sitting on a shelf in the garage. Or it may be something that you know you have an unhealthy attachment to. Remember, as you let go you are learning the practice of emptying yourself. As you let go of the things that you find worth in, God will fill that void.

Write down the item(s) you are going to give away:

_____

_____

_____

_____

_____

     Emptying ourselves of material possessions has a double benefit. First, it creates room for God in our hearts and souls. Another benefit is that we can bless others. As you have chosen your items to give away, now think about who you can give them to. Pray and ask God if there is someone on your heart. If there is no one in specific, you can always give it to a local shelter, ministry, or your church. **In the space below, write who you are going to give your items to.**

_____

WEEK 3
DAY 21

"Be still and know that I am God"
Psalm 46:10

As we finish this third week of our study on the "End of Me", today we are going to take some time to reflect on what God has been teaching us.

Take some time and go back through the past 6 days of this journal.

What is one thing you have learned about God this week?

_____

_____

_____

_____

What is one think you have learned about yourself this week?

_____

_____

_____

_____

What is one thing you can start to implement in your life in order to move toward the end of you?

_____

_____

_____

_____

Today we are going to end our third week of this "end of me" study through a centering prayer. Centering Prayer is a method of silent prayer that helps us to experience God's presence within us. This type of prayer focuses on receiving and resting in God rather than regular active modes of prayer. Through regular active prayer we speak our thoughts to God. Centering Prayer emphasizes prayer as a personal relationship with God and as a movement beyond conversation with Christ to communion with Him.

The goal of this type of prayer is to experience the indwelling of God on a deep level, by emptying your mind of every thought, emptying yourself of every word, and preparing your body to receive by being completely still and silent.

Spend some time in prayer, focusing on being filled by God. Follow the steps below as you pray.

1) Take 2-5 minutes to sit down in a comfortable position. Take deep breaths as you quiet your mind and thoughts. With every exhale, visualize yourself becoming more and more empty of thoughts.

2) Spend the next 5-10 minutes being as still and silent as you can. Focus in on the word FILL, and visualize God's presence filling you.

3) Spend the last 2-5 minutes thanking God for filling you and refreshing you with his presence, and asking him to help you stay focused on his presence throughout your day.

WEEK
FOUR

WEEK 4
DAY 22

*"Many of those who believed now came
and openly confessed what they had done."*
Acts 18:19

In Genesis 3, we read about the entrance of sin into the world and consequently the fall of man. You probably know the story, God told Adam and Eve they could eat of any fruit in the Garden of Eden except the tree of the knowledge of good and evil. One day Eve is deceived by the serpent and eats some of the fruit. She also gives some to Adam and they both disobeyed God. And because of that everything changes. And one of the most important parts of the story happens next. Verse 8 tell us that all of a sudden they heard the sound of God walking in the garden. The verse goes on to say, "and they hid from the Lord God among the trees of the garden." Some theologians say this is the saddest verse in the Bible. For the first time, humanity hides from God. They hid because they were aware of their sin. They hid because they felt guilty and ashamed. From the very first sin, humanity hid from God and we have been hiding from him since.

Read Genesis 3:6-10. In the space below answer the following questions.

What stands out to you from this story?

_____

_____

What do you learn about Adam and Eve from verses 7 -10 ?

_____

_____

_____

What do you learn about God from verse 9?

_____

_____

_____

We too have fallen short. We too have sinned. We too feel the weight of guilt and shame. So we also hide. We hide behind facades we have created. These masks are mere projections of us. We project a certain image to people. An image we want them to see. We project ourselves better than we are. It's just our way of hiding.

In order to come to the end of ourselves, we must realize that we hide. You project a different images of yourself for people to see. Just being honest with that fact is a huge step towards authenticity.

Listed below are different areas of your life. Take some time on each and ask God to help you be honest. Also ask God to reveal to you the truth in each area. When you are ready, write down the image you want people to see in each area. You may want to ask yourself, how do I want people to see me in this area? How do I distort reality in this area so people would see me as better than I am? What do I try to keep from people in this area? Answering these questions will help you see how you are projecting a façade in each area.

Family

_____

_____

_____

Work/School

_____

_____

_____

Friends

_____

_____

_____

Social Media

_____

_____

Gym

_____

- -

Neighbors

_____

_____

Church

_____

_____

Spend a few minutes in prayer, understanding that God knows all this already. Pray and thank him that he still loves you. Ask him to help you understand how he loves you just the way you are. Pray that his love would lead you to put your masks down and be more authentic with him.

DAY 23

"And I pray that you, being rooted
and established in love, may have power,
together with all the Lord's holy people,
to grasp how wide and long and high
and deep is the love of Christ,"
Ephesians 3:17-18

We all have our own image of God. This picture is comprised of many thoughts, ideas, and emotions which makeup our view of God. This image has been comprised over many years and through all our experiences. Our view of God is a very important part of coming to the end of ourselves.

Take a few moment and just think about your current image of God. Be as honest as you can. Do you believe God loves you and wants to know you on a deep level? Do you feel God is on your side or do you feel he is against you? When things go wrong in your life, do you automatically assume God is punishing you or that you did something wrong? **As you reflect on your image of God, write in the space below any negative views of God you have. Where do you think these negative views came from? How do these negative views affect your ability to be authentic with Jesus?**

_____

_____

_____

_____

_____

_____

In the space below, write down the word "Father God" and immediately start to write down whatever words or ideas come to mind. Record any thoughts or images that come to mind. Write down what feelings the idea of "Father God" evokes in you.

_____

_____

_____

Now, in the space below, write down the word "Jesus" and immediately start to write down whatever words or ideas come to mind. Record any thoughts or images that come to mind. Write down what feelings the idea of "Jesus" evokes in you.

_____

_____

_____

_____

_____

Take some time and look over your observations on "Father God" versus "Jesus." For most people there is a stark difference between the two. Most people seem to view "Father God" more harshly. They view him as distant and cold. They view him as more against them than for them. Interestingly, quite the opposite is true of "Jesus." Most people view Jesus as very relatable and loving. They view him as forgiving, gentle, and graceful. Most people view Jesus as one who is for them.

The problem with these two views is that one of them is incorrect. Let's look at some scriptures to help correct our perspective.

Read John 10:30, Colossians 1:15 & 19. What do you learn about God the Father and Jesus from these verses?

_____

_____

_____

_____

What does it mean to you that God the Father's fullness dwelt in Jesus?

_____

_____

_____

_____

_____

The fact is that God the Father and Jesus are one. What that means is that every positive quality that Jesus possessed is also possessed by God the Father. It means that the love, grace, and warmth that we often associate with Jesus is from God the Father as well. In fact, 1 John 4:8 says "God is love." It does not say that God has love. Or even that God is loving. It says that God IS love. It is in his nature. It is who he is.

How does this change your view of God the Father?

_____

_____

_____

_____

How does this new image of God the Father help you be more authentic with him?

_____

_____

_____

_____

_____

_____

_____

Spend a few minutes meditating on the fact that God is love! Find a quiet, comfortable place to sit. Close your eyes and sit in silence as you focus all your attention on the idea that God is love.

"Here is a trustworthy saying
that deserves full acceptance:
Christ Jesus came into the world to
save sinners--of whom I am the worst."
1 Timothy 1:15

CMD: Critical Moment Decision. This is the moment when you are confronted with a huge decision. It is the moment you are faced with a choice and what you decide can change everything. How we choose to act can make all the difference. It can change the course of our lives.

It was in the spring of 1996. I had taken my mom's car out the night before. Now I was standing in front of my mom as she asked me if I knew anything about the dent on her front bumper. CMD... Critical Moment Decision. Was I going to own up to it or pretend I had no idea? Did she know it was me and this was just a test? I wasn't sure, but I knew how I responded would have huge ramifications.

You have probably had your fair share of critical moment decisions. Maybe you have made some very good decisions in those times. Maybe you have made some poor choices. Today, you will have to make another choice. You see, today you are faced with another critical moment decision.

1 John 1:9 says "If we confess our sins, he is faithful and just and will forgive us our sins and purify us from all unrighteousness." Through his word, God says, "I am faithful. I am forgiving. I will forgive you and purify you. IF…If you confess your sins." Now confessing your sins is about the most authentic thing one can do. It's as real as you can get. And God says, "if you get real with me, I will forgive you and purify you. I will accept you just as you are." So today, you will have the opportunity to confess your sins to God. To be completely honest and open with him. To reveal to him your real self. Will you choose to continue to live in hiding? Will you continue to put on masks? Or will you decide to come to the end of yourself? Will you choose to show him your real self and find acceptance in the real Jesus?

Today we are going to give a confession to God, knowing that whenever we do that, he forgives and cleanses us. Grab a separate sheet of paper. On the top of the paper write "My Confession."

Take a few minutes to reflect on your struggles. Think about all the ways you have fallen short in the past. All the things you try so hard to keep hidden from everybody. Then think about all the things you are currently struggling with. The temptations that maybe you have not shared with anyone. Then write out all those things to God as a confession. Share with him all the ways you have fallen short. Share with him all the things you work so hard at keeping hidden. Tell him the true condition of your heart and soul. Confess to him all that you are not and all that you are.

Remember God knows it all. He just wants to know if you are ready to be real with Him. Remember acceptance is found when we are open and honest with God and our real self meets the real Jesus.

Once you are done, you may fold up your confession and place it somewhere safe. Then spend some time in prayer. Thank God for the fact that he already knew all this about you and loved you the same. Thank him for being the forgiver of all things. Thank Jesus that there is no sin his blood cannot cover. Thank God for the fact that you are already drawing nearer to him as you are more authentic with him.

WEEK 4
DAY 25

"When you were dead in your sins
and in the uncircumcision of your flesh,
God made you alive with Christ. He forgave us all our
sins, having canceled the charge of our legal indebtedness,
which stood against us and condemned us;
he has taken it away, nailing it to the cross."
Colossians 2:13-14

I t is only when we are fully honest that we can be fully accepted. When we live behind masks and half truths we will always doubt our acceptance. This is why we tend to question the love of those who don't know every detail of our lives. Even our closest relationships are in question if they don't know the deepest, darkest parts of our hearts. Although they tell us they love us, in the back of our minds we say, they only say that because they don't know who I really am, or if they knew what I have done or the the things I think, they would not love me anymore. This is why we try so hard to hide those things from everyone. It's also why we look for acceptance and worth in other things, or why we seek the approval of other, which causes us to project a false view of ourselves.

However, when we are truly and brutally honest with our sins and the condition of our hearts, and are still accepted, only then can we believe we are truly accepted. The fact is God knows everything about us and he still loves us.

Read Psalm 139:1-6. How do you feel as you read this passage?

_____

_____

_____

Read Psalm 103: 11-12, Isaiah 1:18, Isaiah 43:25, Micah 7:18-19, John 6:37, Romans 8:1, and Colossians 1:21-22.

What is your first response as you read these verses?

_____

_____

_____

What do these verses teach you about God?

_____

_____

_____

As long as we have been alive, Satan has been telling us that our sin makes us unlovable. He has been whispering his lies in our ears that we are flawed. That we are too broken. That we need to pretend to be people we are not because we will never be accepted as we are. And somewhere along the road, we believed him. We believed that we needed to hide behind the masks and pretend to be people we are not even though in our hearts we know the truth. But God refuses to let us go on like that. He pursues us with an unstoppable love and zeal. Through Jesus he tells us we don't have to live like that anymore. So now we must choose. We can choose to continue to believe the lies or we can put down the masks and find that we are accepted just as we are. And when we experience true acceptance, then not only will we not hide but we will shout out from the rooftops the things we worked so hard to keep hidden because we know nothing can ever make God love us any less.

Grab a blank sheet of paper. On it with big letters write the following words:

LOVE   ACCEPTED   FREE   GRACE   FORGIVEN   BELOVED

When you are done, take out your confession letter to God and unfold it. Take the paper you just wrote the above words on and place it over your confession (you may even decide to glue/tape it over!).

Take some time to reflect on how God has truly accepted you flaws in all. Spend some time in silent prayer. Listen for God's voice and be sensitive to the Holy Spirit moving within you. Remember at this moment the real you is meeting the real Jesus

WEEK 4
DAY 26

"The Lord watches over you—
the Lord is your shade at your right hand;
the sun will not harm you by day,
nor the moon by night."
Psalm 121:5-6

"People don't care how much you know until they know how much you care."

A couple of years ago I was at a conference where I heard these words that have changed my life. The speaker was talking about sharing Christ with non-Christians. He shared how many times Christians only share information or doctrine with others, treating faith as a "head" problem. But we know that faith is a "heart" problem as well.

It is as though all of us constantly have a defense wall around our hearts. It's not until we know someone genuinely cares for us, that we can start to lower our defense. It is when we know we are cared for, that we can start to reveal our hearts. This is true in most things including living and being authentic. It is only when we truly know that God cares for us that we trust him with our hearts. It's only when we start to understand God's care for us that we start to reveal to him our real selves.

Go outside and find a comfortable place to sit. Follow the instructions below.

In the space below, write down everything you see. Try to be as detailed as you can.

_____

_____

_____

_____

_____

_____

Look around for animals. Below write what animals you see, including bugs and birds and write how many of them you see.

_____

_____

_____

_____

_____

_____

If there are trees around, count how many. Also try to count how many leaves are on each tree and write that below.

_____

_____

_____

_____

_____

_____

Spend some time observing God's creation. In the space below write down some of your observations. For example, what is the general sense you get from the animals? Do they seem worried or anxious? How would you describe the mood of God's creation (etc.)?

_____

_____

_____

_____

_____

_____

Read Matthew 6:25-34. Jesus tells us that God knows every one of his creation. He knows exactly how many animals are around you right now, even the ones you can't see. He knows exactly how many leaves are on each tree around you. He know exactly what each of the animals, trees, flowers, etc., that are around you need and he cares for and loves each of them. And he knows everything about you. He knows every little detail. And he supplies your needs and cares for you even more than his other creation.

How does it make you feel that God is so aware of all his creation?

_____

_____

_____

_____

_____

_____

How does this exercise make you feel when it comes to being honest and accepted by God?

_____

_____

_____

_____

_____

How does knowing that God is watching over you encourage you to be more authentic?

_____

_____

_____

_____

_____

_____

*"So Jesus said to the Jews who had believed him,
'If you abide in my word, you are truly my disciples, and
you will know the truth, and the truth will set you free.'"*
John 8:31-32

S ome of the saddest stories I have heard center on newly freed slaves after the abolition of slavery in the United States. As you know, slavery was a cruel and corrupt part of the history of the US. In 1863, President Abraham Lincoln enacted the emancipation proclamation stating that all slaves were to be set free. Following suit, in 1865 Congress decided this inhumane practice would no longer be a part of this great nation. Soon after, slaves all over the south were freed. Most of the freed had never experienced freedom as they had been born in slavery. For the freed, it was a reality that they could not have even dreamed of.

History tells us that soon after they had achieved their freedom, many of the freed returned to their plantation and asked for their old positions back. The stories tell of ex-slave after ex-slave giving up their freedom once again to their previous slave owner. Although these men and women had been granted freedom, they returned because slavery is all they had ever known.

Galatians 5:1 says, "It is for freedom that Christ has set us free. Stand firm, then, and do not let yourselves be burdened again by a yoke of slavery." Just like the slaves, we too have been set free from our slavery. The Bible tells us we were once slaves to sin, but we have been freed by Christ. For many of us, we end up going back to being slaves to sin because it is all we have ever known. We must fight every day not to fall back into that kind of living.

In many case, what we are slaves to is our need to present false images of ourselves. To present ourselves in a less than truthful light. We must remember that our freedom lies in the fact that God has accepted us, with all of our faults and failures. The only way to keep from going back to that type of living is to walk closely with God.

Read Galatians 5:16-25. Answer the questions below.

Based on what you know about the Holy Spirit, how does walking by the spirit help us not gratify the flesh?

_____

_____

_____

_____

_____

How are the negative traits mentioned in verses 19-21 indicative of a person who is living a false life?

_____

_____

_____

_____

What are some ways to "walk in step" with the Holy Spirit so you don't go back to put up a facade?

_____

_____

_____

_____

Read over the following Psalm. Once you are done reading it, go back through and look for two things: **1) Underline any word** or phrase that reveals some of God's character, **2)** circle any word or phrase that speaks of the results of walking with God.

PSALM 1

Blessed is the one
who does not walk in step with the wicked
or stand in the way that sinners take
or sit in the company of mockers,

but whose delight is in the law of the Lord,
and who meditates on his law day and night.

That person is like a tree planted by streams of water,
which yields its fruit in season
and whose leaf does not wither—
whatever they do prospers.

Not so the wicked!
They are like chaff
that the wind blows away.

Therefore the wicked will not stand in the judgment,
nor sinners in the assembly of the righteous.

For the Lord watches over the way of the righteous,
but the way of the wicked leads to destruction.

In a sentence or two, summarize this Psalm in the space below. Be sure to use the words you underlined and circled in your summary.

_____

_____

_____

_____

Now it's time to go on an actual walk with God. Plan out the route of your walk. Figure out the midway point of your walk. The first half of your walk is going to represent your walk with God up until now. The second half of your walk will represent your future walk with God.

Remember, you are not walking alone. You are walking with God. So as you walk, try to visualize God being right there with you. Imagine him walking right there next to you as a friend would walk with you. As you imagine him walking next to you, talk to him. On the first half of your walk, talk to him and thank him for being with you until this point. Talk to him about what you've enjoyed on your journey with him. Just share you heart with him. On the second half of the walk, tell him how you would like to walk closer with him in the future. Share with him how you would like him to support you in your walk. Make a commitment to him to walk with him closer than ever.

WEEK 4
DAY 28

"For I know the plans I have for you," declares the Lord, "plans to prosper you and not to harm you, plans to give you hope and a future. Then you will call on me and come and pray to me, and I will listen to you. You will seek me and find me when you seek me with all your heart."
Jeremiah 29:11-13

A s we conclude our study on the "End of Me", today we are going to take some time to reflect on what God has been teaching us.

Take some time and go back through the last 6 days of this journal.

What is one thing you have learned about God this week?

_____

_____

_____

What is one think you have learned about yourself this week?

_____

_____

_____

_____

What is one thing you can start to implement in your life in order to move toward the end of you?

_____

_____

_____

_____

_____

What is the greatest lesson you have learned from this study?

_____

_____

_____

_____

How has this study helped you to come closer to the end of yourself?

_____

_____

_____

_____

As we conclude our study, we are going to pray a prayer that followers of Jesus have been praying for centuries. It is the prayer that Jesus himself taught his disciples. It is often referred to as the Lord's Prayer.

The Lord's Prayer deals with a lot of different issue. Below each line is a question that applies to your life. Spend the next 10-15 minutes praying through the Lord's prayer. Pray going one line at a time telling him where you need that particular quality right now in your life.

"Our Father in heaven,
How close do you need God to be right now?

hallowed be your name,
Where do you need him to be honored in your life?

your kingdom come,
Where do you need God to rule in your life?

your will be done,
In what area do you need God's control right now?

on earth as it is in heaven.
Where do you need encouragement right now?

Give us today our daily bread.
How do you need God's provision right now?

And forgive us our debts,
In what area do you need God's grace right now?

as we also have forgiven our debtors.
Where do you need God's strength right now?

And lead us not into temptation,
Where do you need God's guidance right now?

but deliver us from the evil one."
What do you need God to rescue you from right now?

NOTES

NOTES